...And a little child shall lead them.

Isaiah 11:6

Best-Loved Bible Verses
for Children

Illustrated by
Anna Marie Magagna

Platt & Munk, Publishers/New York
A Division of Grosset & Dunlap

Library of Congress Catalog Number: 82-80877. ISBN: 0-448-46626-0.

The Lord's Prayer

Our Father, who art in heaven,
Hallowed be Thy name
Thy kingdom come
Thy will be done on earth,
As it is in heaven.

Give us this day our daily bread.
And forgive us our trespasses,
As we forgive those who trespass against us.

And lead us not into temptation,
But deliver us from evil.
For Thine is the kingdom,
And the power,
And the glory. Amen

Make a joyful noise all the earth!
Let the heavens be glad,
Let the earth rejoice
Let the oceans roar and all that fills them...
The trees of the wood shall sing for joy
Before the Lord.

Psalm 98

Thou made the moon to mark the seasons;
The sun knows its time for setting.
Thou makest darkness and it is night.

Psalm 104:19

I look at the heavens,
the work of Thy fingers,
The moon and the stars Thou
hast established...

Psalm 8:3

The Lord in His wisdom made the earth...
At His word the seas broke forth,
And the clouds drop down the rain.

Proverbs 4:3

He forms the mountains and creates the wind...
And treads on the heights of the earth.
The Lord is His name.

Amos 4:13

Oh Lord, how many are Thy works.
In wisdom Thou have made them all;
The earth is full of Thy creatures.

Psalm 104:24

He changes times and seasons,
And gives wisdom to the wise.
He reveals deep and mysterious things.

Daniel 2:21

The Lord is my refuge and my light.
Of whom shall I be afraid?

Psalm 27:1

The Lord is good to all.

Psalm 145:9

He has made us.
We are His people.

Psalm 100:3

You cause the grass to grow for the cattle,
And plants for man to cultivate
That he may bring forth food from the earth.

Psalm 104:14

How great are His signs!
How mighty His wonders!
His kingdom is an everlasting one.

Daniel 4

Blessed be the Lord,
Who alone does wondrous things.

Psalms 72:18

In everything give thanks.

1 Thess 5:18

For everything there is a season,
And a time for every matter under heaven.

Ecclesiastes 3:1

The Twenty-Third
Psalm

The Lord is my shepherd,
I shall not want;

He maketh me to lie down in green pastures.
He leads me beside still waters;
He restores my soul.
He leads me in paths of righteousness for
His name's sake

And lo, though I walk through the valley of
the shadow of death,
I will fear no evil;
for Thou art with me;
Thy rod and Thy staff will comfort me.

Thou preparest a table before me
In the presence of mine enemies;
Thou annointest my head with oil,
My cup runneth over.

Surely goodness and mercy will follow me all
the days of my life;
And I shall dwell in the house of
the Lord forever.

Ask, and you shall receive.
Seek, and you shall find.
Knock, and it shall be opened to you.

For everyone who asks, receives;
And he who seeks, finds;
And to him who knocks, it shall be opened.

Matt. 7:7

In peace I will lie down and sleep
For it is the Lord who keeps me safe.

Psalm 4:8